> Greetings from Genius and Success. We are going to develop right attitudes and success characters in our life. Welcome to learn along with us to have smart mind, self–esteem, positive mindset, self-discipline, sharpening our talent and making the right decisions.

My Name is Genius

My Name is Success

Genius & Success
Power of success within your child

Heri Marco

Copyright © 2020 Heri Marco

All rights reserved.

ISBN: 9798647887160

DEDICATION

This book is dedicated to all children.
Bravo, you are the best! See our greetings in our next page

CONTENTS

1. Lion Attitudes
2. Hippo & Water
3. Power to Choose
4. Traffic Signs
5. Never Give Up
6. Parental Guides

INTRODUCTION

READING AND USING THIS BOOK

This is a child self-development guide. The book is for children from the age of 3 up to 12 years old. During these stages, a child's brain greatly benefits from make believe affirmations which builds a strong foundation for intellectual thinking. This is the best stage to build success attitudes and positive thinking in your child. These success attitudes have been practiced by many successful people around the world. However, the main challenge is that most people get to learn the secret behind these success attitudes much later in their adult lives. Those who have discovered this secret have started imparting the knowledge to their children from a young age by instilling success attitudes in their minds. These success attitudes help build self-confidence in children, helping set the stage for high academic achievements, a happy home life and a brighter future.

This book is designed to help your child to build five success attitudes. Assist your child to form a habit by affirming the positive words every day by using Parental guides provided in chapter 6.

- Assist your child to understand his or her life purpose and what he or she is good at.
- Assist your child to read, affirm and make a daily habit to build strong success attitudes.
- Encourage your child to work on these activities until he or she adopts these success attitudes.

POWER OF SUCCESS WITHIN

The power of success within you is your ability to discover your inner qualities and make things happen. Everyone is born with the power of success. This book will guide you on how to develop the five power of success qualities from within.

LIFE DREAM

A Life dream is something you desire to achieve in your life.

Who do you want to be?
- Do you want to be a business man?
- Do you want to be a professional footballer?
- Do you want to be medical doctor?
- Do you want to be a successful musician?
- Do you want to be a soldier?
- Do you want to be a teacher?
- Do you want to be a farmer?
- Do you want to be the president of your country?

SUCCESS

Success is achieving the desired life dream that is beneficial to you, the community, and the nation.

LION ATTITUDES

A positive mindset is the ability to look at something or situation with winning attitude. It is seeing the good in every situation.

POSITIVE ATTITUDES OF LION

One day Genius and Success went on a family trip to visit Mikumi National Park in Tanzania. Once they arrived in Mikumi they boarded a green Game safari vehicle to start their scheduled tour through the park. While touring the park, their tour guide suddenly spotted a lion chasing a buffalo. Genius and Success quickly moved from where they were seating to the open top of the Game Safari vehicle in order to get the best view and watch lions hunting the buffalo. This was a very interesting experience and the following discussion ensured between Genius and Success.

Discussion between Genius and Success

Genius: Why, the lion is small but can hunt the buffalo?
Success: The Lion has a positive attitude. The Lion believes that it can hunt any animal.
Genius: What is the meaning of positive attitude?
Success: It means a winning attitude or success attitude.
Genius: Ohoo! That's great. Me too, I have a positive attitude.
Success: Yes, Every child has a positive attitude.
Genius: So we are born to succeed.
Success: Yes, we can do anything we want.

Genius: Yes, I can read and write
Success: I can sing and play
Genius: Yes, I can do well in my studies
Success: Excellence is our birthright because God made us better than animals.
Genius: Yes, we can do anything, more than the Lion.
Success: Anything we want to do is possible.
Genius: Thank you Success, you are the best.
Success: Thank you Genius, you are great too.

What Next?

While they were discussing, the lion roared, "gruu, gruu". Looking on the far side, a pride of lions were approaching the area where the buffalo was being fought by the hunter lion. Scared, Genius and Success quickly got off the roof of the Safari vehicle and went back to their seats where they could only view the lions through the vehicle window. After a few minutes, the hunt was over as the lion overcame the buffalo and started eating it, joined by many other lions who had come for the food. After this memorable experience, the driver-guide drove the whole family back to the hotel.

Affirmation and practices (guided by parent / guardian)

Genius and Success believe every child has a positive mindset, like themselves. Every child is capable of achieving great things in life if groomed well. Use the affirmations listed below and repeat every day; morning, afternoon and evening with your child / children for best effect to build a mindset shift towards positive thinking.

1. I am born to succeed
2. I am born to do anything I want
3. I am the best
4. I can read and write
5. I am very smart
6. I can do my own homework
7. I am good with numbers
8. I am very talented
9. I have great loving parents.
10. I think positive, therefore have positive, empowering experiences.
11. I have good friends.

Parent/guardian

Help your child to read, affirm, and work on building positive attitudes. Monitor your child and reward for achievement by using the parental guides.

HIPPO & WATER

Talent is a natural ability to be good at something

HIPPO ABILITY TO LIVE IN WATER AND LAND

On the second day, Genius and Success visited the artificial Hippo pool located within the Mikumi National Park. They saw many Hippos swimming lazily in the muddy water. In the area near the Hippo pool, were also many monkeys who were freely playing around with people. One monkey almost snatched a camera from a nearby tourist. It was an interesting interaction to experience. The following were a conversation between Genius and Success while at the hippo pool;

Discussion between Genius and Success

Genius: Success, how many hippos are there in the pool, can we count them?
Success: Yes Genius, let's count…1, 2, 3, 4, 5…. I see 12 hippos in the pool.
Genius: Yes, there are 12 hippos. They have ability to live in water and land.
Success: Yes, that is their natural ability. It is a special talent.
Genius: Ohoo, You mean talent is to be good at something.
Success: Yes, Good news is that, everyone is born with talent.
Genius: Ohoo, that's why I'm good at swimming.
Success: Yes, but you need more with practice to become the best.
Genius: Ohoo, just like how you practice reading and writing until you become the best.
Success: Yes, I am good at writing Genius.
Genius: That's why my teacher says you are the best in writing.
Success: Yes, I want to be a successful book author one day.
Genius: You are the best Success. You will be a successful book author.
Success: Thank you Genius, you will be a successful swimmer
Genius: Thank you, Success.

What Next?

After the discussion, Genius and Success continued driving around the Mikumi park up to the Mkata river flood plain, together with their parents and the driver guide. Within the park, success and genius learnt about different types of trees like the African baobab, acacia and many others. They also learnt about wild birds like the marabou stork, cattle egret and other wild animals like impala, giraffes and zebras. After a long drive, they later went back to the hotel where they had their favorite meal comprised of chips and barbequed chicken, topped with green veggies.

Affirmation and practices (guided by parent / guardian)

Genius and Success believe every child is born with talent. Every child is good at something. Affirm and work every day with your child by repeating the following affirmations to bring out your child's talent;

1. I am born with talent
2. I am good at ……………………………………
3. My parents say I am good at ……………………
4. My teachers say I am good at ……………………
5. My friends say I am good at ……………………
6. I believe I am good at……………………………

Parent/guardian

Help your child to read, affirm, and work to recognize his or her talent. Monitor your child and reward them for achievement by using the parental guides.

POWER TO CHOOSE

A decision is a power to choose. Being poor or rich is a result of a decision.

GENIUS AND SUCCESS DECISION

The third day came with another spirit of adventure. Genius and Success took a day to relax at the Mikumi Safari logde. This is an African style crafted lodge. Its roof is built by using grass. The walls are built by using trees and mud. Genius and Success enjoyed playing and seeing beautiful views and colored butterflies. In the evening they sat at the fireplace and discussed about their adventure of the day. The following was a discussion between Genius and Success at the lodge;

Discussion between Genius and Success

Genius: I like this adventure. I can feel the nature.
Success: Yes, this is because we made the right decision to come here.
Genius: Great, next time we choose only the best to explore again.
Success: Yes, we have so much freedom of choice in our life. We can choose to be successful in anything we do, be rich and live a happy life.
Genius: I understand. Yes, we can.
Success: I choose to be successful and I accept only the best in my life.
Genius: I choose to be rich and enjoy a wonderful life and also help others to succeed too.
Success: I choose best friends like you my brother, who have positive words.

Genius & Success

Genius: I choose the best and durable toys for more learning and to enjoy playing.
Success: I choose to respect and listen to my parents.

What Next?

After the long discussion, Genius and Success went for dinner. They enjoyed their favorite meal comprised of chips and barbequed chicken, topped with green veggies. Genius and Success were then informed by their Dad that today marks the end of their trip and they should get prepared for return to Dar es Salaam, the following day.

Affirmation and practices (guided by parent / guardian)

Genius and Success believe every child can make a sound decision. You are good at making decisions. Affirm and work every day in following to make decisions:

1. I choose to be successful.
2. I choose to be rich.
3. I choose to go to school.
4. I choose best friends who have positive words like me.
5. I choose healthy snacks and meals.
6. I choose to respect and listen to my parents.
7. I choose to respect and listen to my teachers.
8. I choose to read my books.

Parent/guardian

Help your child to read, affirm, and work on decision making attitudes, even small actions count. Monitor your child and reward them for achievement by using parental guides provided at the end of this book.

TRAFFIC SIGNS

Self-discipline is being able to manage yourself. It is a self-management skill.

TRAFFIC SIGNS AND SELF DISCIPLINE

The fourth day came, Genius and Success started their journey back to Dar es Salaam from Mikumi Safari Lodge in Morogoro. On the way to Dar es Salaam, Genius and Success asked their Dad and Mum many questions about the signs along the road. The following was a discussion between Genius, Success and their Parents;

Discussion between Genius and Success

Genius: Asked Dad," why are you driving so slowly Dad?
Dad: I am driving slowly because am following the road sign speed limits, you see, this area is limited to 50 KPH *(Kilo meter Per Hour)*.
Success: But there are no police. You can drive fast now, we miss home.
Dad: Yes, there is no police but I must follow road signs for our safety. We don't obey because of police, we must obey at all times because it is the right thing to do.
Genius: That means you're teaching us self-discipline.
Dad: Yes, that is what a great Dad does. I must set the best example for you.
Success: Good, that means self-discipline is to manage yourself
Dad: Yes, Success
Genius: Now I understand, I will manage myself and obey all rules because it is good to obey rules.
Success: Yes, we must obey all rules because they are meant for our benefit.
Mum: Good job Genius and Success. I'm happy you have got Daddy's lesson right.

What Next?

Genius, Success and their parents arrived in Dar es Salaam late in the evening. Though they were very tired, they had very good memories from the long trip.

Affirmation and practices (guided by parent / guardian)

Genius and Success agreed to manage themselves by practicing self-discipline. Are you willing to manage yourself? Make the following affirmations every day together with your child to help build your child's self-discipline;

1. I follow my home timetable.
2. I follow my parent's instructions.
3. I follow my teacher's instructions.
4. I take action to live my positive good words.

Parent/guardian

Help your child to read, affirm, and work on self–discipline attitudes. Monitor your child and reward them for achievement by using parental guides at the end of this book.

NEVER GIVE UP

Persistence is the ability to do things consistently without giving up. It is a self-drive that keeps you going without giving up no matter what circumstance you go through

PERSISTENCE ATTITUDES OF LION

On arriving at home in Dar es salaam, Genius and Success had a warm bath, changed their travel gear and had a nice home-made meal comprised of rice, meat stew, veggies and fruits for desert. They were all still full of memories from their long trip and started discussing the lions attitude at Mikumi National Park. The Lions hunting formed a great part of the memorable trip, which led to the following discussions;

Discussion between Genius and Success

Genius: Why was the lion taking so long to hunt the buffalo?

Success: Yes, it took almost two hours, a long time for sure….but provided a good show for us to watch.

Genius: It looks like the lion would not give up.

Success: Yes, if the lion gave up there would be no food for him and his family.

Genius: Ahaa, So everyday lions do not give up to hunt because that is how they get their food.

Success: Yes, lions must hunt regardless of how long it takes so that they get their food to survive in the jungle.

Genius: Wow! I have learnt a great lesson from the lion by making sure I keep on doing what I have to do until I succeed.

Success: Yes, we cannot give up until we succeed in anything we want to achieve.

Affirmation and practices (guided by parent / guardian)

Genius and Success agreed not to give up on anything they want to do until they succeed. Are you willing to help your child to develop persistence in order to get what they want in life? If yes, work on practicing the affirmations below with your child every day to develop persistence attributes;

1. I do not give up until I get what I want.
2. I do not give up until I finish my homework.
3. I do not give up until I answer all questions.
4. I do not give up until I finish my physical exercise.
5. I do not give up until I get high grades in my academics.
6. I do not give up until I become the best in reading to my class

Parent/guardian

Help your child to read, affirm, and work on persistence and self-esteem attitudes. Monitor your child and reward them for achievement by using parental guides provided at the end of this book. Feel free to add other affirmations you feel is good for them to adopt.

PARENTAL GUIDES

Monitoring & evaluation guide.

MONITORING AND EVALUATION GUIDE

Use the following guide to assist and monitor your child to develop a solid personal success character.

Positive Mindset

Area	Reward (Excellent, Good, Average, Bad)	Remark
I am born free to excel in anything I set my mind to.		
I am the best of the best		
I am enough! I cannot compare to any other, I am enough.		
I am an amazing person		
I love myself, I love everybody and everybody loves me		
I am brave.		
I am a leader.		
I show empathy and kindness to others		
I choose to have a great day every day.		
My parents love me and I love and respect my parents		
I am a good listener, I listen to my parents and teachers.		
I am creative and very resilient		

Talent Recognition

Area	Reward (Excellent, Good, Average, Bad)	Remark
I am very talented		
I am proud of myself and my achievements		
I am good at :::::::::::: (your child should mention with your assistance)		
My parents says I am good at............................		
My teachers says I am good at............................		
My friends says I am good at............................		

Decision Making

Area	Reward (Excellent, Good, Average, Bad)	Remark
I choose to be successful.		
I choose to be rich.		
I choose to go to school.		
I choose best friends who have positive words like me.		
I choose to eat healthy snacks and meals.		
I choose the best and durable toys.		
I choose to respect and listen to my parents.		
I choose to respect and listen to my teachers.		
I choose to read my books.		
I choose to play safe games.		

Self-Discipline

Area	Reward (Excellent, Good, Average, Bad)	Remark
I am willing to manage myself.		
I follow my home timetable.		
I follow my parent's instructions.		
I follow my teacher's instructions.		
I take action to live my positive good words.		
I live the right decisions I make.		

Persistence

Area	Reward (Excellent, Good, Average, Bad)	Remark
I do not give up until I get what I want.		
I do not give up until I finish my homework.		
I do not give up until I answer all questions.		
I do not give up until I finish my physical exercise.		
I do not give up until I get high grades in my academics.		
I do not give up until I become the best in reading to my class.		
I am strong, smart and very resilient		

ABOUT THE AUTHOR

Heri Marco is the author, researcher and entrepreneur. He is the founder and CEO of Research and Development Network, a company that fosters innovation, advances partnership, nurtures entrepreneurship, translates research into real-world application, and promotes radical thinking professional connections. He is the author of 3 X 7 X 21 Success Formula, The Digital Success Power of Influences, Success Architect, Smart Teens, and Debt is Dirty! The Loan is Clean!

www.ingramcontent.com/pod-product-compliance
Lightning Source LLC
Chambersburg PA
CBHW051941210526
45473CB00006B/2335